LIN-MANUEL MIRANDA

Lights Up

STAGE STARS

Volume 3

A Children's Biography by
Christine Dzidrums

LIN-MANUEL MIRANDA

Lights Up

STAGE STARS
Volume 3

A Children's Biography by
Christine Dzidrums

CREATIVE MEDIA, INC.
PO Box 6270
Whittier, California 90609-6270
United States of America
www.creativemedia.net

Cover and Book design by Joseph Dzidrums
Front cover photo by Helga Esteb / Shutterstock.com
Back cover photo by Lagron49 / Dreamstime.com

ATOS Book Level: 7.2   AR Points: 1   Confirmation #: 1186164
Library of Congress Control Number: On File
ISBN 978-1-938438-99-8

For Charlotte and Matt,
because theater kids are the coolest!

TABLE OF CONTENTS

"Ed Koch once said that New York City is where immigrants come to audition for America. That's what happened to my parents; that's what happened to me."

At age eighteen, Luis Miranda left his home in Puerto Rico and moved to the United States. While attending graduate school at New York University, he studied clinical psychology.

One day, a smart, pretty classmate named Luz Towns caught his eye. The two college students began dating and discovered they had a lot in common. Eventually, they married each other in a modest ceremony.

Following college, Luis eschewed psychology and became a Democratic Party consultant instead. In the 1980s, he worked as a special adviser for Hispanic Affairs under New York City Mayor Ed Koch. During his tenure with the famous politician, he also created the Hispanic Foundation.

Meanwhile, Luz stuck to roots close to her college degree. She worked as a clinical psychologist in Manhattan. The hard worker spent a lot of time on custody cases, often interviewing families so she could make recommendations on where the children from broken families should go.

When the husband and wife welcomed their first child into the world, they named her Luz. Six years later, the Mirandas added a son to their family. They called him Lin-Manuel, not realizing then that their baby would one day grow up to change the face of musical theater.

"My family made miracles happen for me."

On January 16, 1980, Lin-Manuel Miranda was born in the Washington Heights area of Manhattan. When he was five years old, the Mirandas moved slightly north to Inwood. During the scorching summer months, the little boy spent time in Vega Alta, Puerto Rico, with his grandparents, where he learned a new language by talking to his relatives and watching *He-Man* and *The Flintstones* in Spanish.

When Lin-Manuel lived at home in Inwood, a woman named Edmunda Claudia cared for him when his parents worked. The mature woman had once babysat his father, and the Mirandas considered her family. She became a surrogate grandmother to the youngster. Years later, he based a character on her for his first major musical, *In the Heights*.

Music was an integral part of Lin-Manuel's life during his formative years. He listened to a wide variety of music, finding value in all of the genres: pop, rock, blues, and more.

Although the Mirandas lived in New York, they couldn't afford to see many Broadway shows. So, the family built a comprehensive collection of vinyl cast recordings that they listened to all the time. Luis loved *The Unsinkable Molly Brown*, while the elder Luz played *Camelot* during lengthy car trips. Little Lin-Manuel liked both musicals, but he also admired *Jesus Christ Superstar*, *A Chorus Line*, and *West Side Story*.

YOUNG LIN-MANUEL

On occasion, the Mirandas treated themselves to a Broadway show. By the time Lin-Manuel reached his teen years, he had seen three major musicals: *Cats*, *The Phantom of the Opera*, and *Les Misérables*. The shows inspired him to start writing original musicals.

Lin-Manuel also admired animated Disney musicals. He could watch *The Little Mermaid*, the 1989 film based on Hans Christian Andersen's tale of a headstrong sixteen-year-old mermaid who yearns to be human, over and over. The little boy was obsessed with *Mermaid's* flavorful score, especially Alan Menken and Howard Ashman's Oscar-winning calypso tune, "Under the Sea."

"I just remember when that song started, like, this feeling of almost vertigo," he later told *ABC News*. "That was like the most contemporary thing I'd ever heard in a Disney score. I just couldn't believe what was happening. And it just made the bottom of the ocean feel like the coolest place on earth."

One afternoon, Lin-Manuel's sister took him to see *Beat Street*, the music-filled movie centered on New York City's hip-hop culture. The film's heralded soundtrack introduced the youngster to an exciting genre bursting with stylized music set to rhyming speech. Soon, he began listening to albums by The Fat Boys, Beastie Boys, and Eric B. & Rakim.

The youngster devoured song lyrics with unbridled en-thusiasm. He possessed a keen memory and retained even the most complex verses. Sometimes unsuspecting visitors to the Miranda home would be treated to Lin-Manuel serenading them with songs, like "The Twelve Days of Christmas."

Lin-Manuel channeled his love for music into piano lessons. At age seven, he hosted his first piano recital. When the youngster finished his performance, he delighted in the audience's applause. So, he played a second piece and a third. Before he could perform a fourth song, his teacher gently ushered him off the stage so the other students could play their works, too!

The youngest Miranda attended Hunter College Elementary School on Manhattan's Upper East Side. Many felt it was harder to get into the historic school than to gain admission to Ivy League colleges. The youngster noticed that most of his classmates were quite wealthy.

"All my friends lived on the Upper West Side or the Upper East Side, and I'd speak to their nannies in Spanish," he later told *The New Yorker*.

Around the same time, Lin-Manuel developed a passion for performing. The child often recorded videos of himself reenacting movie scenes or lip-synching to pop culture's most famous songs. On one memorable occasion, he dressed as Kevin Bacon's character in the 1984 film *Footloose* while rocking out to the title song.

Lin-Manuel's practice paid off handsomely. In sixth grade, he snagged the title role in the musical *Bye Bye Birdie*. Inspired by Elvis Presley's highly-publicized 1957 draft into the army, the high school staple tells the story of rock 'n' roll heartthrob Conrad Birdie's heavily-publicized "last kiss" on *The Ed Sullivan Show* before heading off to war.

"My abuela made my gold-lamé jacket," Lin-Manuel recalled to *The New York Times*. "Every girl in the grade had to pretend to be in love with me, and I went, 'Well, this is the best thing that's ever happened to me.'"

Little did he know that the best was yet to come.

"[Rent] gave me permission to write about my community. [It] whispered to me, 'Your stories are just as valid as the ones in the shows you've seen.'"

By the time Lin-Manuel had reached his teenage years, he was attending Hunter College High School. During his freshman year, he auditioned for *The Pirates of Penzance* and beat out a senior for the lead role. The talented adolescent also captured parts in school productions of *Oklahoma*, *West Side Story*, *Fiddler on the Roof*, *The Wiz*, and *Peter Pan*.

On Lin-Manuel's 17th birthday, his girlfriend took him to see the Broadway production of *Rent*. Jonathan Larson's rock musical, based on Giacomo Puccini's *La Bohème*, about starving artists struggling to survive in New York City during the AIDS/HIV epidemic, fascinated the young man. He relished seeing a musical with characters singing contemporary songs to express their feelings. The show further inspired him to pursue his artistic dreams.

"Oh, I can do that," he later told *The New Yorker*. "You are allowed to write musicals about now."

Lin-Manuel quickly realized that he enjoyed writing as much as performing. During his junior year of high school, he wrote a 15-minute musical about a Freudian dream called *Nightmare in D Major*. Classmate Chris Hayes, who would later host a news and opinion television show on *MSNBC*, directed the work. He followed it up with *Seven Minutes in Heaven*, a musical about a seventh grader's first kiss at an unchaperoned party.

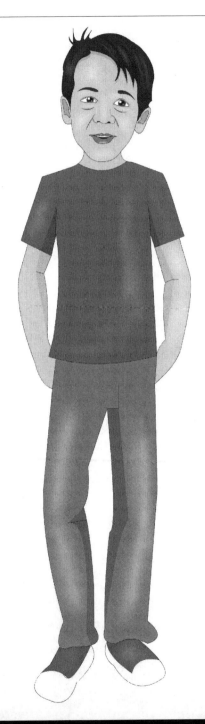

TEENAGE LIN-MANUEL

Sometimes the teenager sat in his school's courtyard during lunchtime clutching his boombox. He often found himself watching a pretty sophomore named Vanessa Adriana Nadal. She acted differently than the other students. The confident girl didn't care about being popular the way his classmates did. She was too busy studying for tests. He always searched for the courage to talk to her, but he never found it.

Following his high school graduation, Lin-Manuel began attending Wesleyan University, a private college in Connecticut. Although the excited freshman initially majored in film and theater arts, he eventually focused all his efforts on the stage. Ultimately, he won the lead role in the school's production of *Jesus Christ Superstar*.

In Lin-Manuel's second year of college, he moved into La Casa de Albizu Campos. The young man lived with eight other students in the cultural center intended to build community among Latino students. It was his first experience making friends with other Latino classmates.

"Just like *Rent* gave me permission to write musicals, this gave me permission to write about home," he told *The New Yorker*.

While living at La Casa, Lin-Manuel felt inspired to write a new show called *In the Heights*. The 90-minute angst-ridden musical told the story of family and friends navigating life in Washington Heights. In the spring of 2000, it ran for an entire weekend at the '92 Theater.

Two years later, Lin-Manuel presented an original work for his senior project. Wesleyan's Center for the Arts hosted another musical he wrote called *On Borrowed Time*. The piece wasn't received as enthusiastically as *In the Heights*, but the fledgling composer had developed a small fan base that turned up to watch his latest show.

Following his college graduation, Lin-Manuel began working as a substitute teacher. He also taught seventh-grade English for a year at his alma mater. During his free time, he revised *In the Heights* after a former college classmate, Tommy Kail, expressed interest in mounting a production of the show in New York.

From 2002-2005, Lin-Manuel wrote five drafts of *In the Heights*. He eventually transformed it from a 90-minute show into a two-act musical. The lead character, Lincoln, was scrapped, and a shop owner, named Usnavi, became the show's narrator. Through his eyes, audiences observed the characters' intertwined lives.

After five workshop presentations, a rewritten *In the Heights* opened in July of 2005 at Connecticut's National Music Theater Conference. While performing the piece in front of a new audience, the composer had an epiphany that changed the direction of the musical. The show's heart didn't revolve around two lovers; it centered on Usnavi's love for his neighborhood. Once again, the show's writer set to work fine-tuning the musical.

Later that summer, craving a break from endless rewrites, Lin-Manuel visited the social networking website *Facebook*. While there, he stumbled upon a page for Hunter College High School graduates. Also registered for the page? Vanessa Nadal, his enigmatic classmate with whom he had never found the courage to spark a conversation. The intelligent woman had recently graduated from MIT and worked as a scientist at Johnson & Johnson.

Determined to meet her, Lin-Manuel sent Vanessa a private message, inviting her to attend a performance of his improv rap troupe, Freestyle Love Supreme. To his surprise, she attended the show, but he felt too shy to talk to her afterward.

A few weeks later, Lin-Manuel summoned the nerve to invite her to another performance. That time, he finally overcame his shyness, and they chatted easily for a long time. The evening ended at his apartment with a fierce game of *Grand Theft Auto*. After acknowledging their special connection, the enamored pair became boyfriend and girlfriend a week later. They have been inseparable ever since.

"I think that being a writer helps me be a better actor because I'm thinking a lot about what the writer had in mind for the character."

In early 2007, *In the Heights* opened Off-Broadway at 37 Arts. Lin-Manuel played Usnavi in the production that ran for 182 regular performances. Audiences loved the show with the big heart, and a strong word of mouth propelled it into a big hit.

"Parents are bringing their children, schools are buying out entire houses at matinees, and senior citizens are coming and connecting to the show as well," the musical's producer Jeffrey Seller gushed to *Playbill*.

On July 26, 2007, producers announced that *In the Heights* would open on Broadway at the Richard Rodgers Theatre. Lin-Manuel wanted to pinch himself in disbelief. His show was heading to the Great White Way, and he would play the lead in it, too!

When *In the Heights* premiered on Broadway eight months later, most critics praised the ambitious work. In particular, *Variety* showered lavish praise on Lin-Manuel's poetic, intricate lyrics. After the performance, the show's star celebrated his Broadway debut with family, friends, and cast mates at a lively party at Chelsea Piers. When *The New York Times* review rolled out, the guests' festive mood only intensified.

"As you watch Mr. Miranda bound jubilantly across the stage, tossing out the rhymed verse currently known as rap like fistfuls of flowers, you might find yourself imagining that this young man is music personified — a sprightly new Harold Hill from the barrio, where this sweet if sentimental musical is set," raved critic Charles Isherwood.

Lin-Manuel felt floored when *In the Heights* received 13 Tony Award nominations, including his two nods for Best Original Score and Best Performance by a Leading Actor in a Musical. The critical darling also would compete for Outstanding Musical against *Cry-Baby*, *Passing Strange*, and *Xanadu*. In all, the show received more nominations than any other show that season.

On June 5, 2008, with Vanessa by his side, Lin-Manuel arrived at Radio City Music Hall for the *62nd Annual Tony Awards*. Hosted by Whoopi Goldberg, the event attracted stage luminaries like Alec Baldwin, Glenn Close, Liza Minnelli, and the original cast of *Rent*.

IN THE HEIGHTS POSTER

AN ILLUSTRATION OF LIN-MANUEL AS USNAVI IN IN THE HEIGHTS

Lin-Manuel tried to remain calm when singer-songwriter Duncan Sheik walked on stage to present the award for Best Original Score. Could the kid from Inwood win a Tony Award? Alan Menken, Howard Ashman, and Glenn Slater, the musical talent behind his favorite Disney movie, *The Little Mermaid*, were also nominated.

"And the award for Best Score goes to *In the Heights*," Sheik announced.

"I used to the dream about this moment. Now, I'm in it," Lin-Manuel rapped in the opening of his acceptance speech. He went on to thank his family, friends, Vanessa, the producers, cast, and crew.

By the night's end, *In the Heights* scored four Tony awards, including the big prize, Best Musical. In addition to Best Score, it took honors for Best Orchestrations and Best Choreography. Plus, the company's energetic performance of "In the Heights" and "96,000" electrified audiences in the theater and at home.

Ultimately, *In the Heights* ran on Broadway for 1,184 regular performances before it closed. Throughout the musical's long run, it welcomed a variety of notable replacements including *American Idol's* Jordin Sparks and *High School Musical's* Corbin Bleu. A producer of the show's Original Broadway Cast Recording, Lin-Manuel also earned a 2008 Grammy for Best Musical Show Album.

Ultimately, *In the Heights* was an undeniable success. That's a mighty impressive accomplishment for a composer's first professional musical.

LIN-MANUEL LAUGHING AT THE MOANA PREMIERE
(Jean_Nelson)

"I gravitate toward music that tells a story."

YOU'RE GONNA CHANGE THE WORLD
Chapter Four

Lin-Manuel had a series of excellent opportunities after *In the Heights'* success. In 2009, he worked with legendary composer and lyricist Stephen Sondheim translating song lyrics into Spanish for a Broadway revival of *West Side Story*. The in-demand talent also appeared on *Sesame Street, The Electric Company, Modern Family*, and *How I Met Your Mother*.

In September of 2009, Lin-Manuel turned his attention toward the small screen with a guest-starring role on *House*. He played Alvie, the title's character's roommate at a psychiatric hospital. The episode entitled "Broken" won the Writer's Guild Award for Episodic Drama. Later that season, the popular Tony winner returned for another episode.

On September 5, 2010, Lin-Manuel and his longtime girlfriend, Vanessa, married one another in Staatsburg, New York. The ceremony took place at the Belvedere Mansion overlooking the Hudson River. The bride wore a stunning Oscar de la Renta gown, while the groom serenaded his newlywed with a production number set to *Fiddler on the Roof's* "To Life," co-starring the bride's family and friends who had spent a month working on the presentation.

In 2012, Lin-Manuel appeared as Charley Kringas in Encores! staged concert of *Merrily We Roll Along* by Stephen Sondheim. Colin Donnell, Celia Keenan-Bolger, and Elizabeth Stanley also starred in the production.

LIN-MANUEL AND VANESSA WALK THE RED CARPET
(Helga Esteb / Shutterstock.com)

LIN-MANUEL AND HUGH LAURIE ON HOUSE
(Fox)

"When you sing the music right, you have very little work to do as an actor," he told *The Associated Press*. "It's like doing Shakespeare — say the words loudly and clearly, and it will pull you through emotionally."

Later that year, *Bring It On: The Musical* opened for a limited engagement on Broadway. Based on the hit film, the high-energy musical tells the story of a high school cheerleader who sets her heart on winning the National Championships. Lin-Manuel co-wrote the music and lyrics with Tom Kitt and Amanda Green. The lively work received a Tony Award nomination for Outstanding Musical.

In 2014, Lin-Manuel added another award to his trophy shelf when he and Kitt captured an Emmy for an original composition for the *2014 Tony Awards*. In the delightful number, host Neil Patrick Harris opened theater's biggest night promising a "Bigger" show than ever. References to *Matilda*, *Pippin*, *Newsies*, and other musicals appeared throughout the wildly popular song.

BRING IT ON: THE MUSICAL POSTER

On November 10, 2014, Lin-Manuel and Vanessa's lives changed forever. Their son, Sebastian Miranda, entered the world at 7 pounds, 10 ounces. He was born in the same hospital as Lin-Manuel.

The new father adored his additional responsibilities. He often sang him goodnight lullabies and wrote an original composition that listed every important person in his baby's life. As his child grew, so did the length of the song!

The talented artist felt on top of the world. He felt immensely grateful for his great blessings in life, like his wife and son. And in a few months' time, he would experience the biggest success of his career.

LIN-MANUEL AT THE OSCAR WILDE AWARDS
(Helga Esteb / Shutterstock.com)

*"Genre is just the clothes
the artist puts on."*

In the summer of 2008, Lin-Manuel went on vacation in Mexico when he picked up an Alexander Hamilton biography at Borders to read while lounging in the hotel pool. Ron Chernow's portrait of America's first Secretary of the Treasury fascinated him. The Founding Father's difficult life told an enthralling story with more twists and turns than a daytime soap opera.

ALEXANDER HAMILTON
(Portrait by John Trumbull)

"Something about it just grabbed me," he told *Playbill*. "I picked up the book thinking maybe I'll get a funny song out of it — some jokey-rap thing about the Hamilton/Burr duel. But as I read it, I realized Hamilton's whole life was about the power of words and wouldn't it be great to hear a hip-hop album about how we created this country?"

An orphan at a young age, Alexander Hamilton moved to New York as an adolescent. A voracious writer, he eventually wrote the bulk of the *Federalist Papers* and founded *The New York Post*. Although a scandal likely ended his chance to become United States President, he remained a highly influential politician until his death at the hands of his nemesis Aaron Burr in the infamous duel.

The wheels started spinning in Lin-Manuel's creative mind. Surely someone had already written a Hamilton musical, right? When the writer scoured the Internet, he was shocked to discover that no such work existed.

Lin-Manuel set to work on writing *The Hamilton Mixtape*, a series of songs depicting the life and death of the famous politician. Initially, the composer wasn't sure if he would turn his idea into a musical. Rather, he considered making a concept CD instead. Whatever came of the work, he had a blast writing it.

On May 12, 2009, Lin-Manuel arrived in Washington, D.C., for a tremendous honor. President Barack Obama asked the artist to sing as part of the *White House Evening of Poetry, Music, and the Spoken Word*. Although organizers expected the performer to sing something from *In the Heights*, he opted instead to sing the opening number from *The Hamilton Mixtape*.

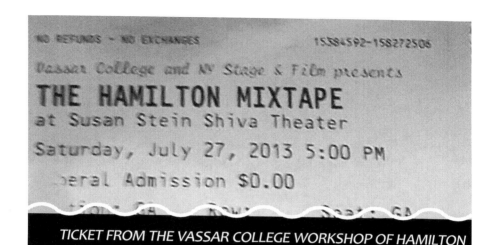

NO REFUNDS - NO EXCHANGES   1SS84592-158272506

Vassar College and NY Stage & Film presents

THE HAMILTON MIXTAPE
at Susan Stein Shiva Theater
Saturday, July 27, 2013 5:00 PM
.eral Admission $0.00

TICKET FROM THE VASSAR COLLEGE WORKSHOP OF HAMILTON

When Lin-Manuel revealed that he was singing a tune from his new hip-hop musical about American history, his statement generated puzzled looks and great skepticism. However, mere seconds into "Alexander Hamilton," the audience became quickly enamored with the song. When he finished the number, the President, First Lady, and everyone else in attendance showered him with cheers and a standing ovation. The composer released a relieved sigh, now certain he was on the right path with the project.

Four years later, *The Hamilton Mixtape* received a workshop presentation at Vassar College's Powerhouse Theatre on July 27, 2013. An eight-member cast presented the entire first act and three songs from act two. During two sold-out afternoon shows, Lin-Manuel performed the title role, Daveed Diggs played Thomas Jefferson, and Christopher Jackson portrayed George Washington.

Once again, the show received a rapturous response. The musical's dramatic story, complex lyrics, and electrifying score enraptured the audience. Among those leading the enthusiastic ovation was Leslie Odom Jr., one of Broadway's most promising, young performers.

Lin-Manuel selected a racially diverse cast for the show. Black, Latino, and Asian actors played the historical roles, all known to be white.

"This is a story about America then, told by America now," he explained.

Encouraged by the show's enthusiastic reception, Lin-Manuel tightened the musical, and it underwent a name change when *The Hamilton Mixtape* became simply *Hamilton*. Although the show still needed work, the author could finally see a finish line.

On February 17, 2015, *Hamilton* officially premiered Off-Broadway at The Public Theater. Lin-Manuel, Daveed Diggs, and Christopher Jackson returned to the roles they originated in the workshop, while Leslie Odom Jr. joined the cast as Aaron Burr. Renee Elise Goldsberry, Phillipa Soo, and Brian Darcy James also headlined the show.

Audiences flocked to *Hamilton*. The show sold out every seat before its first performance and extended its run three times. Meanwhile, critics were equally wild for *Hamilton* with the show earning unanimous raves.

"The sheer scope of what Mr. Miranda crams into his precisely but exuberantly chiseled lyrics is a marvel," raved Ben Brantley of *The New York Times*.

The Guardian's Alexis Soloski gushed, "If (Hamilton) were alive today, he'd have a tough time ignoring the cheers and shouts and wild applause that greet Lin-Manuel Miranda's canny and exuberant *Hamilton*, a fiercely original and dynamically quotational musical at The Public Theater."

It came as no surprise when producers announced that *Hamilton* would open on Broadway on August 6, 2015, at the Richard Rodgers Theater. The Off-Broadway cast would reprise their roles with one exception; Jonathan Groff replaced Brian d'Arcy James, who had previously committed to the musical *Something Rotten!*

ILLUSTRATION OF LIN-MANUEL AS HAMILTON

Again, critics raved about *Hamilton*, and audiences clamored to see it. It became the hottest show in town. Jokes about the difficulty of obtaining a ticket to the musical seeped into the mainstream media.

Even celebrities experienced trouble getting *Hamilton* tickets. However, the show still saw its share of prominent audience members. Jennifer Lopez, Jimmy Fallon, Oprah Winfrey, Tom Hanks, and Will Smith showed up on different nights. Meanwhile, President Obama took in a matinee performance, and First Lady Michelle Obama exclaimed, "It was simply, as I tell everybody, the best piece of art in any form that I have ever seen in my life."

After one *Hamilton* performance, Lin-Manuel met an excited audience member who had loved the show. The theater patron? J.J. Abrams, the writer/director that Disney had entrusted to helm *Star Wars: The Force Awakens*, the sequel to the insanely popular *Return of the Jedi*. Easily the most anticipated film of 2015, the movie would reunite original stars, Harrison Ford, Carrie Fisher, and Mark Hamill, for the first time in 32 years. Everyone expected the film to smash box office records when it premiered in late December.

"If you need a cantina scene, some cantina music, let me know," Lin-Manuel joked.

He felt floored when the director accepted his offer. The two artists began an email correspondence where they collaborated on a tune that would play in the background of a bar owned by a new character named Maz Kanata. Like most *Star Wars* fans, Lin-Manuel eagerly awaited the film's release.

"I'm hoping to be there opening night," he told *Vulture.com*. "I'm going to be very tired at the show the next day, but I'll be with the *Star Wars* gang."

Later, when asked how he found the courage to ask Abrams if he could write a *Star Wars* song, the persistent artist offered valuable advice.

"Ask the thing you want to ask your hero while your hero is in front of you," he urged.

In early March, President Obama invited the *Hamilton* cast to the White House. The talented ensemble hosted a student workshop, a question-and-answer session, and sang selections from their show. Afterward, Lin-Manuel and the President retreated to the White House Rose Garden for a freestyle rap session.

LIN-MANUEL AND PRESIDENT OBAMA FREESTYLE
(The White House)

CROWD OUTSIDE THE RICHARD RODGERS THEATRE
(Jerry Coli / Dreamstime.com)

"You think that's going viral?" President Obama asked the composer when they finished to wild applause. "That's going viral."

On April 18, 2016, Lin-Manuel received another tremendous honor. *Hamilton* earned the Pulitzer Prize for Drama. It marked only the ninth time in history that a musical won in the category. Past winners included *A Chorus Line*, *Rent*, and *South Pacific*.

"It is a tremendous honor to even be considered for this very prestigious award. Quiara [Alegría Hudes] and I were elated to have been recognized as finalists for *In the Heights*, so to win today for *Hamilton* is beyond my wildest dreams," Lin-Manuel remarked. "This award is for everyone who has been a part of *Hamilton's* six plus year journey. To be the ninth musical to ever win the Pulitzer Prize for Drama in its 100-year history is truly humbling for all of us. For *Hamilton* to now be in the same company as *Of Thee I Sing, South Pacific, Fiorello!, How to Succeed in Business Without Really Trying, A Chorus Line, Sunday in the Park with George, Rent,* and most recently *Next to Normal* is outside of our own comprehension. Look at where we are. Look at where we started."

Hamilton received additional accolades with the announcement of the 2016 Tony Award nominations. The heralded production received a whopping 16 nominations, setting a record for the most nods for any show in the award's history. The musical's creator earned recognition in the Best Actor in a Musical, Best Book of a Musical, and Best Original Score categories.

LAUGHING DURING A HAMILTON Q&A
(Brooke Pierce / Dreamstime.com)

In all, *Hamilton* received nominations in the following categories:

Best Musical

Best Book of a Musical
Lin-Manuel Miranda

Best Original Score
Lin-Manuel Miranda

Best Actor in a Musical
Lin-Manuel Miranda

Best Actor in a Musical
Leslie Odom Jr.

Best Actress in a Musical
Phillipa Soo

Best Featured Actor in a Musical
Daveed Diggs

Best Featured Actor in a Musical
Jonathan Groff

Best Featured Actor in a Musical
Christopher Jackson

Best Featured Actress in a Musical
Renee Elise Goldsberry

Best Scenic Design of a Musical
David Korins

Best Costume Design of a Musical
Paul Tazewell

Best Lighting Design of a Musical
Howell Binkley

Best Direction of a Musical
Thomas Kail

Best Choreography
Andy Blankenbuehler

Best Orchestration
Alex Lacamoire

HAMILTON DOMINATES THE TONY AWARDS
(Lagron49 / Dreamstime.com)

"It's unbelievable – it's absolutely humbling and incredible," Lin-Manuel told *The New York Times*.

On June 12, 2016, *Hamilton* ultimately won a staggering 11 Tony Awards. Stage and screen legend Barbra Streisand was on hand to present the show with Best Musical, while Lin-Manuel took home trophies for Best Book of a Musical and Best Original Score. Meanwhile, Leslie Odom Jr., Renee Elise Goldsberry, and Daveed Diggs captured acting awards. Finally, the show's costumes, lighting, direction, choreography, and orchestrations also earned honors.

However, a tragic event the previous day in Orlando, Florida, weighed heavily on the minds of those in attendance. At a popular gay nightclub, a disturbed man entered the premises and took the lives of 49 people and injured 53 others. When Lin-Manuel accepted his award for Best Original Score, he honored the victims with an emotional speech.

"Love is love is love is love is love is love is love, cannot be killed or swept aside," he declared tearfully.

Television newscasts and websites prominently featured the composer's emotional speech. He later joined forces with actress/singer Jennifer Lopez to release a single called "Love Make the World Go Round." Proceeds from the song benefitted the survivors of the Orlando tragedy.

Eventually, all good things must end. Lin-Manuel played his final performance as Alexander Hamilton on July 9, 2016. His last show caused a frenzy among theatergoers seeking a ticket. Some ticketholders paid as much as $20,000 to witness the beloved entertainer take his shot on stage one last time. Audience members included such notable names as Secretary of State John Kerry, actress Jane Fonda, Jennifer Lopez, and director Spike Lee. *Facebook* also live streamed his curtain call.

When the performance ended, Lin-Manuel sported a tired but exuberant smile. He felt ready to move forward to new artistic challenges. To punctuate the point, he chopped off the ponytail he had sported while playing Alexander Hamilton.

'Teach 'em how to say goodbye...' he captioned on *Instagram* under a photo of his shorn locks.

"Art is not measured by the trappings that people attached to it. It's the thing itself."

In the summer of 2015, Walt Disney Animation Studios announced that Lin-Manuel had written several songs for their newest animated film. *Moana* tells the tale of a Polynesian teenage girl who, with the help of a demigod named Maui, sets out to save her people.

Lin-Manuel felt honored to win the writing assignment. A lifelong fan of Disney movies, he had always wanted to write an animated film score. To prepare for his job, the composer sought advice from many Disney legends, including, *Frozen* director Jennifer Lee and the director of the first two *Toy Story* movies, John Lasseter. He felt especially ecstatic to meet Ron Clements and John Musker, directors of *The Little Mermaid*, his favorite Disney film.

"It was a little nerve-racking," he told *People Magazine*. "But working with Disney itself, what's most joyous about it is what a collaboration it is.

It was very much like writing theater. You don't get into writing theater because you like being alone or protected. You get into theater because you like collaborating!"

Ultimately, Lin-Manuel produced several toe-tapping songs for *Moana*. When he finished, a 90-person orchestra from Los Angeles recorded the lush score.

LIN-MANUEL, HIS PARENTS & NEPHEW AT THE MOANA PREMIERE
(Helga Esteb / Shutterstock.com)

The film boasted a charismatic score with character songs bursting with life. The joyous opening number, "Where Are You?," introduced the audience to the Polynesian world as Moana's father, Chief Tui, explained the island's ways to the young girl.

The title heroine's big solo number, "How Far I'll Go," represented the quintessential "I Want" song, a tradition in musical theater where a character expresses their desire for something near the start of the story. In Moana's case, the youngster dreams of sailing across the sea and providing for her family. Upon the film's release, "How Far I'll Go" became the score's breakaway hit. Young girls everywhere belted the anthem while imagining they were the brave Disney heroine.

LIN-MANUEL & JENNIFER LOPEZ PERFORM ON NBC'S TODAY
(Helga Esteb / Shutterstock.com)

"We Know the Way" might be Lin-Manuel's favorite work in the score. The first song he wrote for the film, it best symbolizes his collaboration with Opetaia Foa'I, the Samoan artist who joined forces with him on several songs. For the tune, each artist composed separate melodies which were combined and accompanied by English and Tokelauan lyrics.

Maui, voiced by Dwayne "The Rock" Johnson, sang Moana's most infectious tune, "You're Welcome." Lin-Manuel found the catchy song the easiest to write because he could build the tune around the actor's voice.

"That was such a joy," he told *The Hollywood Reporter*. "We had so much fun in the studio."

Lin-Manuel's 2017 kicked off with a bang on January 24, when he received an Academy Award nomination in the Best Original Song category for "How Far I'll Go." His competition included two songs from the acclaimed movie musical *La La Land*, Sting's "The Empty Chair," and Justin Timberlake's bouncy dance tune from *Trolls*, "Can't Stop the Feeling."

Lin-Manuel proudly walked the red carpet at the *Academy Awards* with his mother on his arm. Chaos surrounded him. Cameras flashed, fans screamed, and reporters begged for an interview. He felt thrilled to share the surreal experience with his mom, whom he had once promised to take to the Oscars if he were ever nominated.

"It's a dream come true for him," a proud Luz told a reporter. "From the time he was tiny, we watched the Oscars."

Several people asked the new Oscar-nominee about his chances of achieving the EGOT – the rare feat of winning an Emmy, Grammy, Oscar, and Tony Award. Lin-Manuel only needed an Academy Award to reach the impressive milestone. Not surprisingly, the humble composer took the question in stride.

"You can't worry about that because you have no control over it," he remarked with a nonchalant shrug. "Why would you spend time on that? I'm good no matter what happens."

In the end, the juggernaut named *La La Land* won Best Original Song for its haunting "City of Stars." Nevertheless, Lin-Manuel seemed content with a nomination, and he enjoyed the opportunity to attend such a prestigious event. At the after-party, the excited artist rubbed elbows with Seth Rogen, Sara Bareilles, Martin Short, James Corden, and more. It was a swell time at the Oscars!

In other news, The Weinstein Company acquired the big-screen rights to *In the Heights*. Additionally, rap mogul Jay Z would produce the film. Those expecting Lin-Manuel to reprise Usnavi on the silver screen were surprised to learn that he would instead appear as a different character in the movie.

"I don't want to play (Usnavi) if it feels like it's not age-appropriate with the rest of the cast," he told *The Huffington Post*.

Lin-Manuel would star in another movie, however. Disney cast him as the male lead in the eagerly-anticipated *Mary Poppins Returns*. Starring Emily Blunt in the title role, the *Mary Poppins* sequel finds the irrepressible nanny visiting a grown Jane and Michael Banks following a tragedy in their life. Lin-Manuel lends support as Mary's friend, a street lamp-lighter named Jack. An impressive cast rounds out the roster:

Meryl Streep, Angela Lansbury, Colin Firth, and Dick Van Dyke.

Although Lin-Manuel now juggled a fruitful film and stage career, he hadn't changed much at all. Despite his enormous success, he remained caring, humble, and generous. Although he was now a role model to many people, he didn't feel much different than the excited little boy who filmed movie scenes on his video camera.

He was always just Lin-Manuel, and that's why so many people admired him.

ESSENTIAL LINKS

Twitter
@Lin_Manuel
@HamiltonMusical
@DisneyMoana

Facebook
facebook.com/Lin-Manuel-Miranda-156195014444203
facebook.com/HamiltonMusical
facebook.com/DisneyMoana

Official Websites
www.linmanuel.com
www.hamiltonbroadway.com

Instagram
instagram.com/hamiltonmusical
instagram.com/disneymovies

Youtube
youtube.com/user/usnavi

Moana
movies.disney.com/moana

Christine Dzidrums has written biographies on many inspiring personalities: *Simone Biles, Clayton Kershaw, Mike Trout, Yuna Kim, Shawn Johnson, Nastia Liukin, The Fierce Five, Gabby Douglas, Sutton Foster, Kelly Clarkson, Idina Menzel* and *Missy Franklin*. Christine's first Young Adult novel, *Cutters Don't Cry*, won a Moonbeam Children's Book Award. Her follow-up to *Cutters, Kaylee: The "What If?" Game*, won a gold medal at the Children's Literary Classic Awards. She also wrote the tween book *Fair Youth* and the beginning reader books *Future Presidents Club* and the *Princess Dessabelle* series. Ms. Dzidrums lives in Southern California with her husband and three children.

www.ChristineDzidrums.com
@ChristineWriter

Theater fans first fell for **Sutton Foster** in her triumphant turn as *Thoroughly Modern Millie*. Since then the triple threat has charmed Broadway audiences by playing a writer, a princess, a movie star, a nightclub singer, and a Transylvania farm girl. Now the two-time Tony winner is conquering television in the acclaimed series *Bunheads*. A children's biography, ***Sutton Foster: Broadway Sweetheart, TV Bunhead*** details the role model's rise from a tiny ballerina to the toast of Broadway and Hollywood.

Idina Menzel's career has been "Defying Gravity" for years! With starring roles in *Wicked* and *Rent*, the Tony-winner is one of theater's most beloved performers. The powerful vocalist has also branched out in other mediums. She has filmed a recurring role on television's smash hit *Glee* and lent her talents to the Disney films, *Enchanted* and *Frozen*. A children's biography, ***Idina Menzel: Broadway Superstar*** narrates the actress' rise to fame from a Long Island wedding singer to overnight success!

BUILD YOUR GYMNSTARS™
Collection Today!

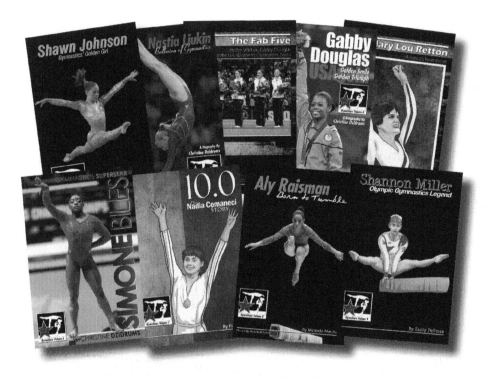

Now sports fans can learn about gymnastics' greatest stars! Americans **Shawn Johnson** and **Nastia Liukin** became the darlings of the 2008 Beijing Olympics when the fearless gymnasts collected 9 medals between them. Four years later at the 2012 London Olympics, America's **Fab Five** claimed gold in the team competition. A few days later, **Gabby Douglas** added another gold medal to her collection when she became the fourth American woman in history to win the Olympic all-around title. The *GymnStars* series reveals these gymnasts' long, arduous path to Olympic glory. *Gabby Douglas: Golden Smile, Golden Triumph* received a **2012 Moonbeam Children's Book Award**.

    Our **YNot Girl** series chronicles the lives and careers of the world's most famous role models. **Jennie Finch: Softball Superstar** details the California native's journey from a shy youngster to softball's most famous face. In **Kelly Clarkson: Behind Her Hazel Eyes**, young readers will find inspiration reading about the superstar's rise from a broke waitress with big dreams to becoming one of the recording industry's top musical acts. **Missy Franklin: Swimming Sensation** narrates the Colorado native's transformation from a talented swimming toddler to queen of the pool.

At the 2010 Vancouver Olympics, tragic circumstances thrust **Joannie Rochette** into the spotlight when her mother died two days before the ladies short program. Joannie then captured hearts everywhere by courageously skating two moving programs to win the Olympic bronze medal. *Joannie Rochette: Canadian Ice Princess* profiles the popular figure skater's moving journey.

Meet figure skating's biggest star: **Yuna Kim**. The Korean trailblazer produced two legendary performances at the 2010 Vancouver Olympic Games to win the gold medal. *Yuna Kim: Ice Queen* uncovers the compelling story of how the beloved figure skater overcame poor training conditions, various injuries and numerous other obstacles to become world and Olympic champion.

Twelve-year-old Emylee Markette has felt invisible her entire life. Then one fateful afternoon, three beautiful sisters arrive in her sleepy New England town and instantly become the most popular girls at Forest Springs Middle School. To everyone's surprise, the Fay sisters befriend Emylee and welcome her into their close-knit circle. Before long, the shy loner finds herself running with the cool crowd, joining the track team and even becoming friends with her lifelong crush.

Through it all, though, Emylee's weighed down by nagging suspicions. Why were the Fay sisters so anxious to befriend her? How do they know some of her inner thoughts? What do they truly want from her?

When Emylee eventually discovers that her new friends are secretly fairies, she finds her life turned upside down yet again and must make some life-changing decisions.

Fair Youth: Emylee of Forest Springs marks the first volume in an exciting new book series.

FUTURE PRESIDENTS CLUB
Girls Rule!

Ashley Moore wants to know why there's never been a girl president. Before long the inspired six-year-old creates a special, girls-only club - the **Future Presidents Club**. Meet five enthusiastic young girls who are ready to change the world. *Future Presidents Club: Girls Rule* is the first book in a series about girls making a difference!

Meet **Princess Dessabelle**, a spoiled, lonely princess with a quick temper.

In ***Princess Dessabelle Makes a Friend***, the lonely youngster discovers the meaning of true friendship. ***Princess Dessabelle: Tennis Star*** finds the pampered girl learning the importance of good sportsmanship.

QUINN THE BALLERINA
The Sleeping Beauty!

Quinn the Ballerina can hardly believe it's finally performance day. She's playing her first principal role in a production of *The Sleeping Beauty*.

Yet, Quinn is also nervous. Can she really dance the challenging steps? Will people believe her as a cursed princess caught in a 100-year spell?

Join Quinn as she transforms into Princess Aurora in an exciting retelling of Tchaikovsky's *The Sleeping Beauty*. Now you can relive, or experience for the first time, one of ballet's most acclaimed works as interpreted by a 9 year old.

What happens when Elise delivers perfect routines but doesn't win? Can the disappointed gymnast accept the silver medal when she dreamed only of gold?

Filled with adorable illustrations and armed with straight-forward storytelling, ***Winning Silver*** stresses the importance of good sportsmanship. Anyone who has ever felt gutted by a competitive result will relate to Elise's initial disappointment over not getting the result she expected.

From the popular new series, ***Classical Reboots,***
Rapunzel updates the **Brothers Grimm** fairy tale with hilari-
ous and heartbreaking results.

Rapunzel has been locked in her adoptive mother's attic
for years. Just as the despondent teenager abandons hope of
escaping her private prison, a mysterious tablet computer ap-
pears. Before long, Rapunzel's quirky fairy godmother, Aiko,
has the conflicted young girl questioning her place in the
world.

Cutters Don't Cry

2010 Moonbeam Children's Book Award Winner! In a series of raw journal entries written to her absentee father, a teenager chronicles her penchant for self-harm, a serious struggle with depression and an inability to vocally express her feelings.

Kaylee: The 'What If?' Game

"I play the 'What If?'" game all the time. It's a cruel, wicked game."

When free spirit Kaylee suffers a devastating loss, her personality turns dark as she struggles with depression and unresolved anger. Can Kaylee repair her broken spirit, or will she remain a changed person?

Made in the USA
San Bernardino, CA
19 May 2018